p-by-Step

Written by Christine Taylor-Butler

Illustrated by Susan Miller

MY First
READER

children's press®

A Division of Scholastic Inc.
New York Toronto London Auckland Sydney
Mexico City New Delhi Hong Kong
Danbury, Connecticut

Library of Congress Cataloging-in-Publication Data

Taylor-Butler, Christine.
  Step-by-step / by Christine Taylor-Butler ; illustrated by Susan Miller.
      p. cm. — (My first reader)
  Summary: When a young boy learns how to make white flowers change color one step at a time, he creates a beautiful bouquet for his grandmother.
    ISBN 0-516-24875-8 (lib. bdg.)   0-516-24974-6 (pbk.)
    [1. Flowers—Fiction. 2. Experiments—Fiction.] I. Miller, Susan, 1956- ill. II. Title. III. Series.
    PZ7.T2189St 2005
    [E]—dc22
                              2005004022

1 2 3 4 5 6 7 8 9 10 R 14 13 12 11 10 09 08 07 06 05

Note to Parents and Teachers

Once a reader can recognize and identify the 48 words used to tell this story, he or she will be able to successfully read the entire book. These 48 words are repeated throughout the story, so that young readers will be able to recognize the words easily and understand their meaning.

The 48 words used in this book are:

blue	eight	I	put	three
can	fill	in	red	two
change	five	it	seven	wait
color	flower	just	six	water
cuts	flowers	love	stems	white
Dad	four	make	step	window
day	get	more	step-by-step	with
days	glass	nine	ten	you
do	glasses	one	the	
dye	how	other	them	

How can I make flowers change color?

I can do it step-by-step.

Step one.
I get two glasses.

Step two.
I fill them with water.

Step three.
I put blue dye in one glass.

Step five.
I get two white flowers.

Step seven.
I put one flower in the blue water.

Step eight.
I put one flower in the red water.

Step nine.
I put the flowers in the window.

Step ten.

I wait three days.

Just one more step!

I love you!

ABOUT THE AUTHOR

Christine Taylor-Butler studied both Engineering and Art & Design at the Massachusetts Institute of Technology. When she's not writing stories for children, you'll find her buried in her mountain of books. She lives in Kansas City, Missouri, with her family and a menagerie of pets!

ABOUT THE ILLUSTRATOR

Susan Miller enjoys illustrating books for children from her studio in the rural Litchfield Hills of Connecticut. Her lively artwork for *Step-by-Step* was created using liquid acrylics on watercolor paper.